The Way We Go On

Acknowledgments

These poems first appeared in the following publications, sometimes under different titles. Thanks to the editors for permission to reprint here.

AACAP Orange Journal: "The Use of Metaphors and Transference"
Another Chicago Magazine: "Ernie's Ladder"
Blue Collar Review: "Tanglewood Mall and the Trickle-down Theory"
Commonweal: "*Miss La La's* Leap from Bible Verse to Modern Verse"
Downtown Tucsonan: "The Quality of Weather"
GLR: "The Way We Go On"
Journal of Poetry Therapy: "Family Photo Album," "Holy Trinity Monastery in St. David," and "A Letter to My Mother after Reading John Keats"
Persona: "Speaking of Lynchburg"
Psychological Perspectives: "What Rain Does" and "Never Mind the Frail Branches"
Therapeutic Recreation Journal: "Games We Learned to Play"
Tucson Citizen: "Fresh from the Trees"
you are here: "When I Think of El Paso" and "At War in Iraq"

Grant money from the Tucson Pima Arts Council and the Arizona Commission on the Arts made the writing of some of these poems possible.

The Way We Go On

For Paul Zarzysky

who introduced me to the poet's life,
"hard knocks and all"

Write on!

Charles

On the Porch of the Governor's Mansion

I used to think my own life
should be like this—
a colonnade of imported
sausage trees drooping,
almost sizzling with fruit
at the edge of Padua Canyon;
a gift, each one,
from the Executive Council
of the Mexican Free States—
planted carefully by ambassadors
who traveled here, riding mules,
crunchy in their winter coats.

But my life, and my life's work,
is more like the fungus
an amateur botanist scraped
from the hooves of those mules.
As he described it,
a sort of black resin
sticky with seeds—and responsible
he believed, for the proliferation
of so many common weeds
spread this far North
from the liberated territories
who were so anxious, first thing,
to barter for peace.

A Gentle Nudge

Walking the neighborhood,
I recognize a strange house
where darkness gathers
in the winter every evening.
Behind a shabby fence
picked clean by the wind,
a picture-glass window
reflects the delicious
departure of daylight
where the gentle nudge
of a street lamp burns.
There is a quietness
curled into the stoop,
folded like a newspaper
and delivered right to the house—
a quietness that sticks
to the shoes of homeless men
who pass and gum the carpets
inside with their silence.

Charles Gillispie

12

Speaking of Lynchburg

Yes, if the station master asks,
sorrow is sufficient
to remove you from this town.

Though his ears are dry as dirt,
tell him your fare is the daily insult
failed love accrues.

Watch his fingers tremble and snap
like the spur in his back
as he peels your ticket
and gives you third class.

You will not escape his cloudy eyes
that learn your face through cataracts.

He predicts the string of all-night diners
draped around your neck
and the vacant motel rooms
flaring up inside of you
like nostrils, burning.

Trust this man:

He understands the odd shape love assumes
as it disappears,
the way his own life disappears,

falling from his face
as he stands at the turnstile
waving to strangers.

The Odd Shape Love Assumes

I stand at the door
after dinner, the way
my grandfather used to:

staring out through a screen
barely visible at dusk,
remembering how he cleared

scraps from our table,
mostly pork bones and gravy—
pitching them over the porch

for the neighborhood dogs.
To the future, he said.
Years after his death,

a whole life I've lived
without my grandfather knowing,
he still brings it back

with his joke, the future I mean,
how little it requires of us—
how little it deserves.

Charles Gillispie

Under the Weight of a Sparrow

My grandmother said Jesus
died in a dogwood tree
and that's why some of the flowers
bloom pink each Spring.
Never mind the frail
branches unable to support
a man dying—weak even
under the weight of a sparrow.

She didn't live long enough
to see uncle Buddy
wither in the limbs,
weak from cancer and a love
for the fiddle, his voice
like a beetle jug
shaping the melody.

He was the last entry
in her Bible, an unplanned
conception—his face tough as tree bark
from the belief
he had inconvenienced her.
That idea left its mark,
driving Buddy to champion
good and hand himself over
to the opinions of others
crackling underneath that weight
like a stick of dry wood.

Games We Learned to Play

Sorry and *Trouble.* *Headache* and *Risk.*
Each board game is a little facsimile
of the mess we make at the end or our street
where Michael chops a bathroom door off its
hinges. My older brother David teases him,
locked inside. My sister Kathy screams
until they quit—typical family scene
together for a summer, alone in
the house. We're best of friends by five o'clock
playing *Risk* in the kitchen when our mother
comes home. We call her over to ask advice
hiding our fear in concern for the dice.
We know her rage—buried like a bone. Just
our luck—how easily it becomes a part of us.

Charles Gillispie

A Letter to My Mother after Reading John Keats

Barbara: I'm eating breakfast this morning
on the patio, underneath the mock-
orange. I have a box of maps beside me
(my way of keeping in touch with family)

and the new edition of Peterson's
Field Guide. As I write this letter, I hear
an English Sparrow crack sunflower seeds
at the feeder. I have my own need

to penetrate the closed surface of things.
Funny how silence, once established, clings.
Most of all I want to hear your story—
especially those years you lived obscurely

with some Private AWOL from the Army
in Texas, around 1963...
I want to hear about the campsite
he made by the river where you slept nights

all summer in love, and later, trouble.
Was that the first time you heard the gentle
curve of water folding into a bank
while stretched in the grass enjoying the dank

odor of leaves and the shape of a man?
What you can't tell I think I understand.
I've been to Texas. I've looked for that place
between small towns along the Interstate—

plenty of room for the silence
strung between us like a barbed-wire fence.
We stand on opposite sides, embarrassed,
talking birds and rivers and county fairs

as if we lived in a different century
when nature still provided transcendence.
Better to describe the Western Tanager
than some scar left from my father's anger—

that Romantic who married you,
who brought us together but pulled us apart, too.
(As we admire nature's artifacts
we forgive his involvement in things like that).

Charles Gillispie

Your Arrival Is My Meal

for S.L.S

Your tongue and my tongue—
butterflies without their shoes
inside the restaurant.

My promise is your napkin.
Your arrival is my meal.

Every Sunday night
another kiss goodbye
and the wind runs home

kinder to strays and hobo
men who damn the elements.

A fish could marry
a bird but where would they live?
The streets are empty

and pigeons understand this
roosting in the public eaves.

Holy Trinity Monastery in St. David

I have only come to study
the customs here
in this hermitage
where twenty-five monks
crowd the wooden tables
and stare at one another
eating cabbages.

Dug deep into the mound
of a century, their eyes
are narrow hallways
lined with portraits
of the fool, their patron
saint—a man who looks
to be mentally retarded,

painted in a frock coat
framed and hung on the wall
where his face
continues to expand
and approximate
the miracle of science.
Alone in his chapel,

I am filled with a visitor's
difficulty, unable to discern
my own lack of knowledge
from the great veil of ignorance
he promises any disciple
wise enough
to follow his ways.

Charles Gillispie

Never Mind the Frail Branches

When the Hooded Oriole
arrives on Tuesday morning,
the sidewalk below
him stops in one place.
The offices empty
and a middle-aged woman
points her finger,
painted at the nail,
attempting to illuminate
his fabled presence
in the branch of a pine tree.

Just then, he drops
and shows his belly—
a flush of lemon scrubbed clean.
His black hood flashes
over our heads
the way stars fall,
inspiring silence
and a lust for beauty—
making him, in this moment,
our monk
and our executioner.

What Rain Does

Under the street lamps,
water stretches a thin
skin across the asphalt—
I follow the sidewalks
and adhere to my perceptions
which wind and flood
into intersections.
Here, I am in the openness
of four directions:
my past, my future,
my mind and my mood.
The rain carries with it
something from each.
I feel properly
collected by the time
my foot is ankle deep
in water at the curb.
Mostly what I seek
is a lost relation.
From the raindrops
born into clouds,
I want to know
and be known by
all who are absent—
shouldered up there
above the earth,
dripping from iron fences,
thirsty for the street.

Charles Gillispie

The God Bag

The surgeon from Seattle
wears it on his hand like a puppet,
sarcastically groping
at his neighbor—
she's only eighteen, on Prozac
but still horny.

A dove calls from the tree
outside, a broken penny-whistle sound
repeated compulsively
as other patients
gather in the Lecture Hall—
uneasy in their flip-flops
and summer shorts—almost goofy
with pride.

We draw the curtains,
burn a candle for atmosphere
and pass around the God Bag.

The basketball player from Houston
places his grief inside the bag,
trying hard to not laugh or cry.

The travel agent from San Manuel
fumbles a bit, still shaky from detox,
but manages to place her marriage
inside the bag.

Forty-five minutes later, it's chock-full
of lost jobs and dead children.

In closing, we all shake hands and hug.

The eighteen-year-old resolves,
tearfully, to become a better person
and then exits toward the pool.

We stay behind to straighten the chairs,
gather tissues and styrofoam cups,
and, finally, toss our God Bag
back into the closet
with all the other games and puzzles.

Charles Gillispie

Sleeping on Doors

Bright as a bedsore,
one red rose
blooms from a clay
pot in the kitchen—
planted by our good friend,
Michael, still

propped in his chair,
beetle-browed
and reeking from the last
days of living.
A blanket of red
tape is wrapped tight

around his neck
like the actual flower
he planted himself
from a seed, blooming
by the sink,
defying the malodorous

rut of herbal supplements
and his frightening
squeal of flatulence.
The history of that rose
confounds me.
I wonder how it survived

the glass of Greek
wine almost black with pine
resin we once poured
into the soil,
ceremoniously...
And all those baseball games

Michael tried to watch,
nodding off, burning himself
awake with a perfectly rolled
joint—his antique sofa
smoldering through the night.
Someone please explain

the roil of fortune—
the good smell of wood
rubbed into the door frames
of this house—the insightful
glimmer of each glass knob
splintering the past

from the present, creaking,
when turned, with a clarity.
Explain please
the door Michael worked so hard
to strip and finish,
how it hangs on its hinges

like all of us, good friends,
unsure to come or go—
resisted daily,
pushed away—merely
a barrier now between here
and some place else.

Charles Gillispie

The Quality of Weather

When I see you under clouds
riding your bicycle
between buildings,
I want you to know your face
takes the ache
out of this asphalt,
already cracked and full of holes.
I'm just sorry
I didn't know you as a boy,
displaced for the first time
in a neighborhood like this one,
scarred from rain and hard wind,
yet flourishing
underneath the jurisdiction
of Nineteenth-Century lamp posts.
I realize how sensitive
you must have been—
becoming a metaphysician,
losing boundaries on a day
like this in cold wind,
fitting yourself
into the meaning of public space.
Even I can read *pigeons* and *absence*
like a kind of grammar
when the smell of French fries
and car exhaust is mixed
with wind and leaves.
As for myself,
what I hold most of my
interest in these days
is the affective
quality of weather
when I'm in it with you.

Family Photo Album

We knew the faces
staring back at us
as two-way mirrors,

pushing the world out
while pulling us in.
We loved those heroes

strung like beads across
the pages of the
family photo album—

an abacus used
for counting the losses
passed along to us

from some ancient hand.
We fingered and picked
the tattered folds,

those missing parts:
the uncle and aunt,
grandparents, father—

retrieving ourselves
from portraits the way
our mother pulled weeds

alone on her knees
all day Saturdays
fenced inside her garden.

Charles Gillispie

When I Think of El Paso

The wind makes an old noise
picking away at loose ends—
the kind of scrap
found in a border-town
bungled-up at the horizon,
a dwarfed plain
full of street life
that lined our bellies once.

Car windows still rattle
in their carriages,
poised to listen:
listen to the Interstate
sweat like a snake—and cringe
at the ruptured bend
of a dipstick losing oil.

That was our story
back then—trapped inside
the accordion folds of a road map.
We made camp on the line
between two countries
and whenever we spoke—the wind
carried our trouble
back into the empty canyons.

Fresh from the Trees

I am lifted by the smell
of turkey in your kitchen,
Father Taft. The Chapel
of the Infant Jesus
is at your mercy: a cookie
in your mouth and a knife
in your hand. How you found
your way to be priest
after forty years of marriage
and a career teaching science
is a miracle worthy of Moses.

Your arthritic fingers,
curled and dove-like,
are the ten commandments
your parish follows
as you open a can of Folger's
on Wednesday night
and roast the heart of our city.

Father, you argue salvation
is a space inside the heart
no larger than the hull
of a thimble. That best explains
your own success
tending to the minor details:
carving meat and blessing children,
standing as you do,
on feet flat and crunchy
as the grass out here
in the churchyard—a perfect place
for a person like me to pause
and wonder at a person like you.

Charles Gillispie

Do Not Bend

You know and I know
he's had his chance out there
in the street dodging cars
and cussing the kids
at Kentucky Fried Chicken
for a free cup of coffee.
Now, the bus stops
and the doors swing on a hinge
open for him,
still standing—advised
by his cohorts: *Do Not Bend.*
He steps up and into the smell
of a stain, the back of his own
pants soiled, sickening
but durable. Yes, he is
fresh from the trees,
that dusty row of bare-ass
branches planted in the alley
between the avenues,
a little forest he can poach.
He rides downtown
nodding-off, unemployable,
sandwiched between the seats
like a piece of bad meat
jerking and turning into the aisles
as if roasting on a spit
as we brush past him quickly
on our way off the bus
seasoning him with *sorry* and *excuse me.*

The Use of Metaphors and Transference

Members of the group
arrive and the ground
between us loosens:
all eight of them
angry to see me
instead of their regular
counselor. Friendly, I call
each one by name,
handing out "shovels."
I instruct the group
to form a line
and start digging.
Like children, they comply—
slicing away, not sure why
yet proud of the distance
between us. I tell a few jokes,
hands in my pockets,
staying in my place
until a man breaks off
from the group.
He jumps the line
and comes at me,
swinging. Nobody sees
where I take him
though we cover every
inch of that office.
Then I stop,
as if in the middle
of an open field,
listening to him pant.
Right there, I ask him to pretend
that I had been his wife.
To just make-believe
it was her instead of me.
I hear the whole group
stop and put their shovels
down, not to watch

Charles Gillispie

a grown man cry
but to observe the thing
they have uncovered:

underneath their anger,
whole families—mouths full of dirt—
still talking
but exhausted from the struggle—
packed in like that
for generations.

A Night at Contentious Ruins

Cold weather strips Autumn from the trees.
Only a crumb is left on the branches
above the San Pedro, soggy with leaves,

but essentially empty. The deficit
fills me with an aptitude:
a complete *gestalt*, undiminished.

Higher up, the sky itself is undiminished—
interviewed by clouds and a moon
yammering into daylight. My thoughts

do the same and I try to keep pace,
adjusting myself like the river—
aware of every mound, every dip

and rise along the edge. Apart
from you, back home, no other creature
troubles me here. There was an owl

last night by the fire, sounding off—
and the cold air, almost crackling.
Except for the wind

infused with its own tendency
to dismantle and make bare,
there is nothing left but you and me—

listening for each other
from separate zones, reduced by distance
to a milder civility.

Charles Gillispie

When Books Were Milestones

for H.E.E.

Dead leaves in the grass
remind me of our friendship
many years ago.

Each leaf is a page
from one of the books you owned
at a time in life

when books were milestones.
Each leaf is a fossil print
of old paradigms

scattered now by wind—
wispy without connections
and freed from their task

of instructing me.
Away from the knuckled branch,
each leaf lies alone

though identical
in a way that cancels loss
and communicates

a brief history
of having served a great purpose—
like you and your books.

Freed from My Task of Instructing You

Back home, stars
mark the distance I travel
from my office to the table.

You pinch a dead leaf
from the plant between us
and empty your water glass

into the soil. I try to explain
how the smallest word
can open a window

and push me through.
Like water from your glass,
I go on and on—

until I find myself
at the end of a dry root
and return to my place

here at the table,
pulled in once again—
eating my dinner with you.

Charles Gillispie

Dreams

If you hold the fossil,
the fossil of who I was then,
you will observe the basic
apparatus designed for defense.
I marvel at the primitive
function. The simple
usefulness. For example,
consider the hand
empty and unencumbered,
free from the modifications
imposed by work or love.
The palm is already wrinkled
into a map of the neighborhood
but its landscape
is unformed and un-made.
Lines in the flesh
run like alleyways
cluttered but fresh,
able to nourish dreams
and pigeons, actual birds—
roosting on wires
and fences, mindful
of themselves only
and the need
to be themselves—which is the same,
of course, as a dream
and the instruments,
like hands, used
to manage dreams.
It's what they refused
as a general defense, those hands,
these hands,
that I'm so proud of now:
what they didn't pick up,
what they wouldn't put down.

A Pageantry Steeped in Aftershave

I watch the young couple
who splash across the street
with a soggy paper
draped over their shoulders
and a laugh
pulled from the headlines.
For them, this is pageantry—
steeped in aftershave
and fabric-softener.
For me, this is business—
out here looking for you
in a rain coat
I wear only five times
a year. If I find
a phone, I promise to stop
and give you a call—
not to apologize
but to ask for directions
back home and a description
of this street
before it filled up
with rain and became
a worn path
back into the underworld.

Charles Gillispie

The Seduction of Pony Boy

Pony Boy rides that bolt of neon
burned into his arm. He is a wet

seed dripping from the barstool, spilling
into the soil of a potted plant.

Upstairs, in the attic, his bedroom
bakes from the day like an iron cage.

The clogged wheels of a fan wobble,
confused as a music box playing

all by itself: blowing him kisses,
wearing him down. He is no stranger

here among the cow-pokes on the wrong
side of town, just too young for this mess

of days and nights, dressed and then undressed
like an envelope pressed through the mail—

and all he really has is a good heart
banded to the leg of some pigeon

flying through the cracks of evening.

Tchaikovsky in the Fingers of a Fool

1.

A small wind is made
to carry the shape of leaves
already plundered

from your piano—a phrase
able to choke or nourish.

Stuffed into the score,
the sound is a dinner roll
tough as a mountain

buttered thick at the edges
in the fingers of a fool.

2.

Now, I am confused:
I address the composer
and blame him for love

hidden inside your body.
I address the musician

and criticize her
for the scent on my fingers
after touching you.

Did you pinch a lemon rind
and rub it into your neck?

Charles Gillispie

3.

The pigeons return
at intermission. Old men
flood the urinals—

I stand outside under trees,
green with sound, waiting for you.

In the last movement,
a peasant smashed a street lamp
and killed a pigeon

with a pistol. I sniff your
leg and feel just as crazy.

Miss La La's *Leap from Bible Verse to Modern Verse*

Casual as a sumptuary law,
Miss *La La* is comfortably

clothed in her refusal to speak
the pluperfect, or God forbid,

the imperfect. Totally dependent
on her use of morphemes,

she spins from the ceiling
of the Baptistery embarrassing

the cloister nuns with a lust
for her revealing lexicon:

her enclitic suffix
barely attached, her accusative

inflections unwept and unprofaned.
Please forgive the desuetude

of her semantics. Though every detail
is open to analysis,

her own smirk is by far
the most reasonable form of prosody.

Charles Gillispie

Thursday

I've put this poem off as long as I can
driving to work—apprehensive—alone
with my thoughts. The shows on talk-radio
belt their empty spleen. I understand
how a puff of hot air can lift you…Traffic jams
the next strip of Interstate and I'm bored—
flipping from news, to Rush Limbaugh, to praise the Lord.
At my office, I welcome the demand—
blinking, first thing, the Help-On Call lines.
Those shaky voices always bring relief.
I find comfort in the crisis they provide,
each one requiring a certain wisdom and ease.
I almost believe it by the end of the day,
driving home, all that confidence in what I say.

I Accept Such Flimsy Notions

As long as the pine needles
crunch under foot, between
here and there, the Clark Fork
packs a tight curve.

Downriver, deer
drag their nostrils
across the emery board—
sipping the swift current.

Fear is hard to ascertain
in creatures so gullible—
like you and me
gliding toward the hills

jammed into the shallows
occasionally—rocks close-knit,
smooth as a tongue
lying in the silt.

The mountain behind us,
without a name yet,
completes an open circle.
Planes fly above the quirky ridges

and we ward off Moccasins
which don't exist here—
but a touch of moss on the ankle
is a ventriloquist

mouthing our phobia. For now,
I accept such flimsy notions—
just you and me, without zip codes,
floating the river.

Charles Gillispie

Summer at the Cable Plantation
in Concord

After dark, we fear
the room John Cable
died in—upstairs
at the end of the hall.
My brother and I
light the wood stove
as early as August
listening to crickets
pull the night apart.

We pump enough copper
from the well to forge
a new penny—fresh water
salty as blood but cold
and quick to boil,
good for the chocolate
and coffee that warms
our walk through the fields
where grass, rough as sandpaper,
brushes our knees.

We are careful to avoid
the water snakes
and the breeding bull
loose on the bank
as we fish the river
all night, needing a break
from John Cable
and his suicide—especially
the leg brace hung from a nail
in his closet,

the shoe still expressing
his foot—conjuring
him back to a place

he despised,
at the top or the bottom
of any stairway
in the house—still
scarred from his walking
and busy with mice.

Charles Gillispie

At War in Iraq

Wind is heaped
against our front door,
rattling the screen.
Inside, we unpack—
our second day
in the new house,
pulling tissue-paper
from our artifacts,
curious to hear
the crinkles echo
into an emptiness
full of possibility.

The dogs sniff
sausage and stick
to my side. You come
for breakfast
with a newspaper
and pat their bottoms
gently. Their ears perk
to the sound of our forks
tapping at the plates
like sword-play.

Without curtains,
we see the street
outside and vow to become
better citizens
watching the wind
brush a new crop of leaves
across the sidewalk
where they gather
in front of our house
like so many reasons
fallen from the trees.

Ernie's Ladder

It's hard to get a good
place in line. Workers crowd
the door like cardboard
cutouts hung from the same
thin wire.

Ernie is the one
with the crack in his face
and the stomach
full of car change. He does
O.K. on $28 a day:
cigarettes, a bag lunch
and a hot cup of coffee
from Circle K.

Ernie sleeps in the office
after they sign him in.
His eyelids rise like a dead man's.
But Ernie isn't dead. He's dreaming
of his toothpick palace
on 22nd Street, and his pocket
sized bedspread and pillow case
full of concrete.

He must be falling in his dream.

His arms and legs twitch
the way blind men
play accordion. Yet Ernie
doesn't make a sound.
If he's not careful,
he won't wake up

before he hits the ground.

Charles Gillispie

Sweet Pea

The retarded man walks
his dog in the park.
The dog, parasitic,
hops on three legs
dumb in the face
like his master. Both,
driven by appetite,
grow into the amorphous
shape of a tumor, uneven
as they walk
and falter in the grass.

As a child,
I might have imagined
a surplus of hope—
always a hand or tongue
to feed each other's
hunger, always an object
to reflect each other's
love in equal portions.

But having left my parents' home
to find my place in the world,
I've learned about portions—
I know if that dog
were more than a dog,
he could escape
his retarded life
and sneak away somewhere
to grow a new leg.

He could surrender
the odd trope of ticks
clumped around his neck—

clean himself up and shake off
the idiot grin at the other
end of the leash
which soaks his brain
like a sponge and provides
the *retardedness*
never really his
in the first place.

Charles Gillispie

A Faith Like Agua Caliente

At one time, you were right with the world,
and the world was right with you—
back in winter of 1999. We drove to Agua
Caliente and walked the lake, early.

The absence of color was appropriate then—
a poverty we shared with the wood ducks
and geese. Any brown tuft of prairie grass
was void as any reed crowding the shallows.

One did not add or subtract from the other,
plain, green lake water notwithstanding...
What did you say that felt so calm—
vague as the cloud cover dampening our day?

Just your look, I guess, rich with a hunger.
Hardly afraid or even embarrassed
by HIV—you pointed to some mountains
worn smooth at the horizon, attempting,

in their own way, to be beautiful.
Wherever you are now,
unable to be moved by the things that move you—
remember that much, from Agua Caliente.

The Mustard Seed Boy's Ranch

I step from the truck with a box of books
as a boy shouts over my head:
We're sick of that mountain—
would you move it?
And the other boys laugh.

Past the pool table
and into the group room,
the boys fight like birds
for the best chair.

Inside the box, the books
smell of grass and old horses.
The boys settle in to sniff
and search for a story
different than their own.

I pass a note pad, like a communion wafer,
and ask each boy to add a line.

At the end, the biggest one,
the joker who got the best chair,
demands to read out loud:

Literature

The books travel everywhere
like a highway at 5pm
stacked tightly together
smells of dead cattle
spirit of live prey
on a mission to be read

with nothing to lose
except a girl I loved in school.

Yee, books is tight!

Charles Gillispie

The frail spines bend
back in contortions
from each county and state
lingering with hatred.

The books reach their suburban
destinations and eat TV dinners
with their kids.

The books are bandits
equipped with masks
and firearms
bound with leather
and golden text
traveling in an El Camino,
ganged up, luring those
who would dare to speak—
loading their words with meaning

but no action as most would guess
the pages useful only when stuffed
into shoes that do not fit well.

Trip-wires abound in their wake.
Through the streets they walk

Thugg'in
Thugg'in

A Kiss Trapped in the Abdomen of a Bee

Jays bully the light
at the base of the mountain—
without a moral.

I come here with their fiction
and your kisses in my mouth.

Small animals flee.
What I carry on my back
is the weight of hope

summoning emergencies
to keep me out of trouble.

Clouds and pine needles
enter the conversation
whenever I leave words out.

My heart is in two places—
with the sparrow and the squirrel.

A string of dead bees
tells the story of desire
floating in the spring.

I linger around the well
but decline to drink from there.

Aspen leaves, also
yellow and dead, ford the gaps
between sun and moon.

Underneath my boots, they pose
riddles for bears and lovers:

Charles Gillispie

Can a kiss trapped in
the abdomen of a bee
crush its will to live?

Sex has an ontology
but love, set aside, does not.

On the mountaintop,
when permitted to be known
wind and lizards part.

The silences keep us close
while blisters widen distance.

I have photographs
of myself on this mountain
surrounded by friends.

In fact, remembering that
illusion inspired this poem.

A Hole in the Carpet

The treadmill at the gym
wets my shoe like a tongue
stuck out for viewing,
or in my case, reflection.
I walk into a mirror
at the back of the throat,
which clears in my presence
like a bit of night air.
In that clarity, I see
my face as a mirror
reflecting my father's face
walking toward me
as fast as I walk toward him.

If the tongue could speak
I might hear his anger
cursing the sales route
he drove for 30 years.
If the tongue could speak
I might hear the guilt
in my own voice
wearing a hole in the carpet
as I talk with my father
on the phone at home,
in love with my job
for 15 years—
but wondering now
whose shoes I'm walking in.

Charles Gillispie

Tanglewood Mall and the
Trickle-Down Theory

Tanglewood Mall sat on top of the hill
above the Interstate—a fresh odor
rose from the grass groomed like carpet.
I should have been hopeful, but I wasn't—
Ronald Reagan won the last election
and Poland was in the news every night

smeared across my fingers black as night
from delivering papers up the hill.
Poland, after the election,
folded like a leaf of boiled cabbage—an odor
that might have fed somebody. But it wasn't
for me to say. Swept under the carpet,

worker's rights wore a hole in the carpet
of my own house. My father stayed up nights
scribbling notes in his route plan. He wasn't
happy driving up and down the seven hills
of the city—a distributor—who owed
his livelihood to the last election,

which gave us everything an election
was supposed to give: a path of red carpet
from the warehouse to the mall—cheap odor
of shirts and pants made in Asia. At night,
signs from the clothing stores lit the hill.
They could charm my father if he wasn't

sleeping—seduce him like a moth if he wasn't
angry—where he stood on the porch elected
democratically to his humble
circumstance. He called me on the carpet
out there—his own way—gentle as the night
air rich with familiar odors

like sausage frying in a pan next door.
I bundled my extra papers though it wasn't
required—a nervous way to pass the night
with my father—while he recollected
the better half of the last century.
His memory brought us back to the hill

when it was just a hill—disordered
carpet of honey suckle—neighborhood landmark—not
worth much more than a promise on election night.

Charles Gillispie

A Similar Romance

Fly little bird—
above the squalor
and the fume.

Your wings, primed
and groomed, increase
the girth of day.

My walk beside
traffic is tangled
in your branch:

trunk of mesquite
dank and tepid,
a portal

your belly opens.
Jesus, when speaking,
did that in red ink

printed on the page,
invoking a similar
romance—

an industry
peculiar as the slope
in your shoulder—

so
sure of the world,
little bird.

An Industry Peculiar as the Slope in His Shoulder

On the bus to Galway, two Germans
shout back and forth from underneath
headsets, seven hours out of Cork
and bored. Tired of fences and farmhouses.
And sheep. I'm stuck with Radio Ireland
blasting through the back of the bus,
advertising a breast implant
made from sugar and water.

Suddenly, there's Dunfanaghy township.
Simple isolation cradles a gale force
terrible at the coast. Here, a woman
boards the bus carrying her baby
and a new broom wrapped in plastic.
Her quiet face reflects the Protestant graves
dug into the hillside above us.
She holds her child steady
as a glass of milk while the bus
bobs and weaves through the narrow street.

Finally, we huddle inside a small kitchen
choked by the peat fire
while an old man complains.
He speaks in Gaelic
and then English, filling his own ear
with an ounce of history
pinched from his arm.
His grandson watches the World Cup on TV
and cheers for the wrong team,
oblivious to British atrocities
three-hundred years past
and still being poured
into the old man's cup.

On the wall behind him,
a field map of County Donegal
is pinned above the stove.
Plain heat from the peat fire
has cracked open the ocean at Horn Head,
dividing the peninsula.
Like the rock fences outside every village,
splits in the map are crude
but effective—interrupting all the rivers
and all the roadways
from Falcaraugh to Londonderry.

In the headlines, ten Catholic churches
burn in the North and John,
a boarder from Belfast,
takes it personally. Upstairs in his room,
drinking Guinness, John pores over
the newspapers, afraid to sit
at the old man's table.
From the bottom of the stairs,
we plead with him to come for tea,
to forgive himself
for nothing *he's* done. But he won't have it.
We hear the cans crack and news
seep like gas from underneath his door.

Irritated, the old man
comes to drag John down the stairs,
through the back door
and out to the pasture behind the house
where they sit and talk for an hour,
the old man with his hand on John's shoulder—
surrounded by the stone fences
built and then neglected and then rebuilt
for so many centuries.

The History of Of

Unable to escape
the law of gravity,
St. John, the Cross,
decided to build
a temple:
for the vault
of his chapel,
he picked through
the carcass of a firecat
and retrieved
the arching spine.
For the legs of his altar,
he chopped off
the arms of a snowman
and planted them
into the ground.
For the door
to his sanctuary,
St. John hung
himself on a rusty
hinge and for the rest
of eternity refused
to open or close.

Charles Gillispie

News

Finally, just to stop
and listen from inside the house,
through the open window.

Our neighbor crushes an aluminum can
at this hour, flattening
the shape of a day.

His wife, I hear, is pinned to the chair—
watching commercials on TV.
Her own voice, when she speaks,

is from Czechoslovakia—
able to twist off the head of a chicken.
The wind picks up

and I'm eager to hear
more news from the world,
but nothing else floats across

the space between our homes—
except the licorice smell of asphalt
rising, quietly, from the street.

How Love Survived the Marriage

He was in business for himself and she winced
when he traded a half day's labor
for an old tape recorder that didn't
even work—as she suspected—another favor
for a friend. He splayed the recorder open
on the kitchen table, arranging the parts
where they sat for months on paper napkins.
It seemed adolescent—how he'd start
to repack the magnet or examine a reel
and then stop, eating around his own mess.
Until the evening she found his recorder
fixed at the table. She gave it a test,
curious to hear his garbled words—but instead—
taped from early morning—the sound of birds!

Charles Gillispie

Liquid Metropolis

I have acquired many things
but not your history—
frail and worn as a sliver of soap
lost to the drain.

I smell the cruel church floors
that lift you up and away
from your own crucifixion.

I see you in the pews on Sunday morning
sucking yellow candy, alone in Zurich
for the first time.

I imagine a crystal ball
in your shoulder bag,
complementing the dusty shadows
that stick to your eyes.

Your passport is brittle in your pocket
and a train serving salad greens
last Saturday is your only true friend
inside this liquid metropolis.

My heart is like a tree
thirsty for your sorrow:

sit with me, quietly,
below the stained-glass windows
and let me love your strangeness,
stranger.

An Introduction to the Future of Mankind

Under the marquee,
my brother and I
stop to watch
the last pigeon flee
from the main street
in a section of town
embedded with cobblestones.

The sidewalks are littered
with popcorn and the smell
of dead leaves burning.
We stand quietly
against the brick buildings
pinched into place:
two-stories high, three-
stories high, side by side.

My brother is a different
story altogether,
reflected in multiple
images at the ticket booth.
He laughs at the woman
who takes his money
and notices the nicotine
stains on his finger,

the oil of Christ
preaching a sermon in his hair,
and his unusual stare
into the future of Mankind
given back
like a receipt
after social transactions.

Charles Gillispie

Salvation Army Hospitality House

All these years I've chipped
away at him, self-absorbed
and self-afflicted, determined to wear
him down: *Fat Charlie the Chronic*,
drowning in his delusion.

Forgive my failure.

Where have I been all this time,
so amused and betrayed
by a lunatic?

Walking the avenue like him,
I suppose—reflected in similar
storefronts, *apprehended*,
lifted from myself anonymously,
and then repelled
with obvious pleasure
by the corresponding street
names and street numbers.

Without a context,
Charlie and I are the same—
troubling each other's space
daily, deprived of our fantasies
by the common sound of our name.

When we meet at intersections
in the city, it doesn't matter
enough to acknowledge.
As long as we pry
our way back into the shelter
each evening, we are familiar all the same—
trapped in opposite roles we both fail
to adequately explain.

The Way We Go On

for B.A.C.

Your hot bath and talcum
powder mark the calendar
Saturday night as you write
me a check for *eight hours*
labor and ask me in for dinner.
I smell food at the door:
oatmeal and salmon
teased into patties
round as pennies on the plate.
I was in your yard all day
spreading a load of gravel,
a pink shell of decomposed
granite colored
like a salmon's belly—
but empty at this hour
and hungry for conversation.
The contours I made
in the yard, we discover
through a tiny kitchen
window at sunset, exaggerate
positive and negative space.
Daylight and gravel
give the same hue
seamless there where shadows
pulse like so many phones
taken off the hook.
The way we go on
about the yard, I think
I am falling in love
with the landscape—
when in fact
I am falling in love
with you.

Charles Gillispie

About the Poet

Charles Gillispie is a counselor who specializes in the use of creative writing as an adjunct to cognitive-behavioral therapy. He has published articles describing his work in *Addiction Professional, Arizona Together, Journal of Poetry Therapy,* and *Therapeutic Recreation Journal.*

Charles has received fellowships and grants from the Tucson Pima Arts Council and the Arizona Commission on the Arts in support of his work with writing and therapy.

He is a founding member of the San Pedro River Pilgrims, a backpacking club dedicated to the pursuit of spirituality through wilderness adventure.

Breinigsville, PA USA
28 December 2010
252308BV00001B/8/P